Folding the Wilderness Within explores the many different and
compelling landscapes within all of us. From a child's *webbed*
hands holding cards to Machu Picchu where *stones fit so tight not
even a hair can pass,* Joan Shillington weaves reality, imagination
and language to form a poetic story *as if filming a movie or a God
watching.* These poems, filled with our humanness unite and
guide us into the future.

Folding the Wilderness Within

by Joan Shillington

 Frontenac House Poetry

Book and coverdesign: Neil Petrunia, Epix Design
Cover photo: Neil Petrunia
Author photo: Heather Shillington

Library and Archives Canada Cataloguing in Publication

Shillington, Joan, 1948-, author
        Folding the wilderness within / Joan Shillington.

Poems.
Issued in print and electronic formats.
ISBN 978-1-927823-11-8 (pbk.).--ISBN 978-1-927823-12-5 (html)

        I. Title.

PS8637.H524F64 2014   C811'.6   C2013-908744-3
                                           C2013-908745-1

Frontenac House gratefully acknowledges the support of the Canada Council
for the Arts for our publishing program. We would also like to thank the
Government of Alberta Multimedia Development Fund for their support of
our publishing program.

 Canada Council **Conseil des Arts**   *Alberta* ◢ Government
for the Arts   du Canada

Printed and bound in Canada
Published by Frontenac House Ltd.
1138 Frontenac Ave. SW
Calgary, Alberta, T2T 1B6, Canada
Tel: 403-245-8588

For Phil (1917-1998)
and Anne (1915-2003)

Contents

Currents   11

The Fifties   13

Evinrude   14

Elna   15

Summer Job 1935   16

The Hunter   17

The Cottage   18

Poaching   19

Family Dinners   20

Portrait of My Mother in Her Kitchen 1942   21

Brownie Meeting   22

A Brown Owl and Her Daughter Walk Home
      in Minus Thirty Celsius   23

Ice Break-Up   24

The Neighbour Speaks from Beyond   25

Dawn   26

Wild Horses   27

Canning Peaches   28

Roll Up the Rim   29

A Bush Pilot Executes His Last Shutdown   30

Cessna   31

Co-ordinates   32

Childhood Westerns   33

My Father Prepares Himself for the Task Ahead   34

Piano Lessons   35

Bringing in the Cattle   36

Au coeur vaillant rein d'impossible:
      Nothing is impossible for a willing heart.   37

Innocence
            for amm   38

On Visiting the Desert After Learning
      of a Friend's Lapse into a Coma   39

Machu Picchu   40

Learning to Drive   41

The Carcass   42

Nightmare   43

Dreams   44

Seasons   45

Midnight Run   46

My Father As Tsar 1946   47

Waiting   48

There Are No Stories In My Family   49

The night my mother died...   50

Summoning   51

My Mother's Sister   52

White Chalk on Slate   53

The Rosary   54

The Gospel   55

Seba Beach   56

There Are No Stories In My Family   57

The Forgetting   58

Beginning the End   59

On Her Eighty-Eighth Birthday,
    My Mother Asks Me to Iron   60

Meditation on Wasps   61

Abduction   62

Remembrance Day   63

The Last Afternoon of My Mother's Life   64

Meanook Cemetery   65

May First   66

After the Funeral   67

Ordinary   68

A Measure of Taste   69

Monopoly   70

Lady Luck   72

He is driving...   73

Caterpillars   74

Acknowledgements   79

Folding the Wilderness Within

Currents

Listen, I say here that stairs lead to a lake.
Steep, forest green stairs. Fathomless.
The type of paint sold at a local hardware store.
Texture without shadow.
After the long absence it is sometimes difficult to recall my mother's face,
or the back of my father's hands,
blue veins traced with child fingertips.
The moon, a full, round bowling ball, weighs me into the stairs.
Owls cease flight.
Buddha says we are what we think.
I think bougainvillea: pink, red, orange, white.
I think endless possibilities.
A deer emerges from the forest into headlight beams.
A pen nib scratches across the blank page.
Once, I was afraid of my father, but now he is gone
and my memories skip, soft and flat as a pebble across the water.

The Fifties

In those days I was their hope, a baby boomer, a child among
adults, a mistake, included in all-night card games, an after-
thought. Seba Rummy, poker, blackjack, hearts. I could hold
fifteen cards as if my hands were webbed, each face and number
visible by a tiny degree of separation. Mom, Dad, Jim and
Lorette, Neil and Betty. Working women with mascara, rouge,
eyeshadow, long painted red nails next to my mother's naked
face and pale fingertips. The men wore their war like a long-
sleeved shirt, flat felled seams on skin, pressed cottons covering
every pore and hair of their upper bodies, liquor transparent as
the bottles they poured from, an antiseptic that swirled fox holes,
night raids and trench mouth into stubby glasses. They spoke
adult: politics, mortgages, moonshine, unions, mechanics.
Ed Sullivan. Small and silent, I was a child with baby adults in
their thirties and forties. By 3 am my eyes burned cigarette ash
and incandescence. Beer kegs balanced on dry ice in wheelbar-
rows. Whiskey and rum bottles littered the counters. My soda
beside their alcohol. Smoked oysters, garlic, cheese and crackers.
Raw onions in white vinegar. I laid my cards on the table with
theirs: pairs, three of a kind, full house.

Evinrude

Once, I was a girl
perched on the back of the driver's seat,
throttle pushed into my palm.
I took that lake fast as those seventy-five horses would go.
My sweet teenage years?
Burlap draped windows,
moonshine dripped into thin-necked bottles.
I flamed one hundred and fifty proof in metal spoons,
sliced elk membrane from out-of-season carcasses,
fur falling wild across my shoulders.
I was the girl who never brought friends home,
who closed the door behind her,
not a glance back at the wake.
And that's life, isn't it Dad?
Barrel assin' through the gilded water,
listening for logs to strike against your hull.

Elna

Afraid of the dark
I wander barefoot
in a long nightgown
through the small hours
and stand beside my mother,
her grey head illuminated
beneath the sewing machine
light, she guides fabric
through the presser foot
with cigarette stained
fingers. Sometimes,
I settle at the kitchen table
in my father's chair
and rest my head
on crossed arms,
the arborite
white and cool.
I listen for his step
on the porch,
red click of the warming oven,
his dinner visible
behind tempered glass.
Eyelids asleep, his
presence lifts me
into his arms, and
then, only then,
my mother releases
the pressure bar,
lips silent-thin
as the sleeping house
serves him.

Summer Job 1935

As she punched groceries through the till,
he navigated among the vehicles
in the garage across the street.
Bent over engines,
stretched on a flatbed beneath,
he worked topless, torso painted in sweat.
She began to picture him naked,
ate lunch on a pine bench,
feet flat on the plank porch,
sipped milk from a quart sealer,
nibbled on a ham sandwich.
Billowed dust from a farm half-ton or
Ford coupe hid him from view.
In this thickness of summer heat, she
lowered her hands to her lap,
held herself perfectly still
and kept her gaze steady.
She did not blink.

The Hunter

A man returns from hunting.
He unrolls his cuffs, loosens boot laces,
spews twigs, leaves, burrs
across the kitchen floor.
Every word he speaks can be held in human hands:
moose rack, rifle, wild meat.
He sits anonymous among all that is his,
the wife who busies herself with broom and dust pan,
children beyond a distant room.
He lays peeled, sweaty socks on the kitchen table,
unbuckles his belt, top trouser snap,
tugs out his shirt, reveals white underwear.
On the counter elk steaks thaw.
In the garage, bones and sinew hang
from a meat hook.
Already, the man has prepared the head for mounting.

The Cottage

From the beginning, the cottage belonged to the mounted heads and stuffed pheasants, as a museum might belong to sculptures, artifacts, paintings, or bed to the teddy bear placed on a child's pillow. But these animals were slain into trophies, glass eyes gazing through dust motes and layered smoke to the opposite log wall. Spiders wove their webs through antlers, feather, talons and each spring they were taken down, hauled outside, sprinkled with baking soda and brushed until shiny. A little housekeeping trick learned from Blue Flame Kitchen. Refreshed for another twelve months. No one gave them another thought until the booze began and egos bragged antler points and gutting methods. The trophies saw it all. Imagine a black and white silent film all those years, people scurrying in and out, drinks tipped to lips, a little girl reading in the brown chair, kitchen table card games, naps on the sofa. The projector crackles and scratches: months, seasons. Years sliver between drapery panels, seconds allotted for each frame. The daughter walks into the room from bright sunlight, blinks into the smoky haze. On the sofa with her father, an unfamiliar woman. Red hair, red nails. He lifts his head toward the daughter, slowly butts his smoke in the overflowing ash tray. Lifts a beer to his lips. Watch her retreat stepping backwards, back, back, farther and farther, she leaves the screen. Fragile celluloid splinters fold over and over on itself: click, click, click. The screen, blank, grey.

Poaching

I always thought it was a bond between us, fish net set just as the sun rays obscured sight. We gunned that Evinrude across Lake Wabamun to Reservation Shore and when the motor cut out, I lowered an oar, pulled the boat forward as my father guided the carefully laid folds over the side, wooden floats bobbing on the surface. In rough weather, engine idling, I shifted in and out of gear, bow pointed into the wind. Each week the cold crept closer and we donned tuques and gloves in our furtive missions as flopping fish were hauled into plastic bins. My father's hands shook with cold as he lifted his drink in celebration. Sometimes we took neighbours and friends along for the adventure, everyone bundled, and, with drink in hand, stepped gingerly from pier to boat, giggling at the possibility of being caught poaching or God forbid, striking a log in the large dark. I don't remember if he set nets again after the accident. All I know is, by the time the ice broke up, he was a single man with a new double-hulled sixteen footer, unsinkable as the one that sank.

Family Dinners

Winters we ate my father's wild game,
taste buds assaulted by tansied bark and muskeg,
infusing our father's barrenness within us.
We listened to him as a hunter hears the land,
each crack and sough a tympanic explosion.
Camouflaged in undergrowth, we stalked elk,
moose and deer, burrs and twigs snapping
at our clothes. Sunlight flashed on birdsong.
Glint of white tail. Brightness and shadow
layered the forest floor, the north of moss.
A kick-back of gun butts muscled
into our shoulders, the lone coyote's guttural
howl into the night as a solitary man slept naked
in eiderdown. With seared steak on the plate
before us, we knew predator and prey. Children
at the table of this feast, refracted
in the crosshairs of his telescopic vision.

Portrait of My Mother in Her Kitchen 1942

She likes the early afternoon sun at her table,
fresh cup of coffee and cigarette.
She knits into this winter warmth.
Two apple pies cool on the counter,
three children down for their naps.

The Allies Losing to Hitler, headline news,
thick with wounded and dead.

A drift of clouds pull shadows through the room.
She pauses in her rhythm of stitches,
sets an unfinished sweater in her lap,
sips from the white porcelin mug,
draws a glow of smoke into her lungs.
Steel needles and clock movement
only sounds in the house.

Brownie Meeting

The table must be perfect.
Sunflower napkin beneath
each knife tip.
A flower beside each glass.
Carnation. Pink.
I want my uniform sleeve filled
with badges, even though
they have to be unstitched
and resewn with each wash.
My Brown Owl mother
makes me sew them myself,
no matter how crooked.

Stir white sauce constantly.
Be patient or it will scorch.

I turn away for a minute
and the pot burns black.
Brownies is held in the basement
of Central United Church each Tuesday.
Ladies at my school, St. Catherine's,
ask my mother to form a Catholic pack.

No. Brownies has to be all denominations.
Not just Catholic.

We walk the miles home together
no matter how wet or cold.

A Brown Owl and Her Daughter Walk Home in Minus Thirty Celsius

Tuqued heads haloed in frost-breath,
fingers fisted in double-knit mittens,
we crunched along snow tracks, tire tracks,
drifts dwarfing us on either side.
Northern lights blazed brighter than stars.
Fushia, gold and orange flamed above us.
I was so afraid the world was coming to an end.
But you stopped me in the middle of our journey,
laid your hand on my shoulder and willed a stillness,
willed that thin, crystalized air to etch Aurora Borealis
into the slate of our universe.

Ice Break-Up

That spring the ice broke up on our shore, shearing piers and boat hoists frozen in the ice. Wind, wild and cold hollowed into our heads and the great ice sheet moved toward land, moaning and groaning, filling the air with ghost bones, crying to us as if from another world, pushing, cracking, piling on banks, half-foot thick slabs grinding, colliding with each other, higher and higher, the weight of the whole lake pushing, pushing, chugging as loud as a train engine, strong, steady ice-squeal, gouging rocks and sand, ripping away from the lake as a great tear, all the fear and longing of the world, lake-soul exposed, upside down, inside out. A heart plucked. It was like that. Fractured air. Knife stab and twist as when a father disinherits his son or mother abandons family. Thunder and crash.

Then there was quiet and the lake lay naked, cold and blue.

The Neighbour Speaks from Beyond

Let me say, this is not how anyone could imagine it is to drown.
August water creeping over my soles, then ankles. Slow list of
boat and there I was, caught between nightmare and reality. I
tipped the last of the twenty-six past my lips then lashed my
wrists to a rope and eased myself across the overturned hull.
Rum burned in my gut as if I had swallowed glass from the
bottle. Haunted voices hurled themselves from a distant

shoreline. Words, distorted, sank. Confused letters on black
water. I counted the seconds between lightening and thunder.
Paper, scissors, rock. Our Father who Art in Heaven. Cold
cleaved my body. I rocked and swayed with waves. I became
boat. Storm. Water. Rain. Soon, I was not seen but could see. I
saw the dark beyond the cottage. Family. Wife. Children. A girl
on the opposite shore who could not come. And now, she has
forgotten my name.

Dawn

In the end, it was dawn that saved us.
That red and orange herald emerged from night,
tamed storm clouds to a low glow on the horizon.
Dawn, threw light carelessly
across the lake as if it were an ordinary day.
A healing salve. Inside the cottage
we breathed hope. Miracles. Whitecaps
calmed with such suddenness we thought
the water would part and expose
our lost boat and people. We opened
windows and doors, invited dawn in.
A strange car pulled into the driveway.
One person, my father, stumbled out.
Bare feet, torn pants, thistles.
He had walked the night and the storm.
We thought hero and turned to one another
with the knowledge. His shadow huddled
at his feet, shivering. There is a price
for deliverence. Dawn, higher, brighter
glanced her radiance at us as a mirror
might reflect a glint: wisdom? pity?

Wild Horses

By 4 am my father and I lift into the wide yawn
of an orange-fringed sky,
head north from Edmonton to Fox Creek, then Jasper.
Deep into the foothills, he suddenly banks right,
drops altitude, prods my shoulder,
motions *look below.*
My stomach lurches as I peer past the wing.
A band of wild horses, frightened by the plane
race our shadow,
hooves cup the muskeg
flay moss in their wake,
sinew, muscle, tails, manes
fluid as a coursing stream
drum into the day
flank to flank,
weaving and leaping
scrub spruce and pine
they part only for boulders and trees.

Canning Peaches

I often think of those Augusts,
sterilzed Mason jars, glass lids, red rubber seals
strewn across the counters.
Okanagan Fruit stamped on stacked boxes.
And my mother,
in a white sleeveless blouse,
shorts and open-toed sandals
cradles the warm, sweet globes in her palm,
exposes butter-orange fruit beneath fuzzy skins.
Floored in the center of a sticky kitchen,
she slips peach slices into sweet syrup.
Sweat beads collect at the base of her throat.
She transfers sealer after sealer to tea towels
spread on the counter. Row after row,
they cool. She returns and turns
them upside down. Tests for a vacuum.
Who was she? This woman? This woman
who still occupies every space of my day.

Roll Up the Rim

Brittle and restless that day, Mom,
you kept shifting your shrunken buttocks
as you balanced on the edge of your last bed.
Lucid and annoyed, you finally order me to Safeway.
the prescribed meds souring your stomach.
Across the street from the funeral home, you said,
fruit flavoured Gaviscol, NOT tablets.
Couldn't harm you at this point, I reasoned.
On the way back I stop for a large Double, Double.
I spoon the pink syrup into your mouth
but you only anxious for my empty cup
and *Roll Up the Rim,* as if winning
a free coffee or cookie would allow you
to rise from your bed,
walk across the highway
and redeem the prize.

A Bush Pilot Executes His Last Shutdown

He knew the end was near. Still, he had bars
installed over all the windows, added
inside bolts. *Too many burglaries,*
he said, although there was nothing to steal,
rabbit ears splayed on the television,
cassette player on the music shelf.

Days lengthened and shortened shadows.
Each night he slid bolt locks in place,
tested bars, executed *The Procedure Checklist*
from pushback to shutdown. White filmed
his eyes, lungs thickened, bones stiffened.
The staccato voice of the air traffic controller
ricocheted through his head:

Alpha, Bravo, Tango. All clear for takeoff.

Cessna

If you had been there you would understand my soft love of cloth, how birdsong punctuated an air of rafters in my father's hangar and how torn strips of flannel nightgowns, white cotton shirts and underwear spilled out a sack he took from the side cupboard. My father showed me how to polish his Cessna, to lightly wipe a folded rag twice the breadth of my hand across the wax and apply a thin layer on a four-by-four square to the waiting surface, then rub to a high gloss, taking care to wipe the excess from around each rivet. Sometimes he spread a tarp beneath the propeller and disassembled the engine, placed parts on the canvas, washed them in varsol, dried and reassembled. Back and forth between his red tool box, each tool in its exact drawer and place. My father taught me to work in an easy rhythm with wide circular movements and not take too many breaks. In the evening his calm voice spilled through the doorway of his office, a woman's laughter tinkled with his rye and water, and I would keep working on his little plane, draw the smell of Simoniz and airplane fuel deep into my lungs. Low lights cast shadows on the immaculate concrete floor, sparrows flitted, chirping above, my arms constant in their movement, slipping through the air and clouds like silk.

Co-ordinates

He knows this landscape best from the air.
Wild ponies galloping beneath the shadow of his plane,
animal indents on snowpack.
From this distance, he follows his snowshoe track
as he carts a mule deer out on his back.
He moves to the window, the wheelchair squeaks.
Everything begins to thin.
Visitor coats drape the hospital bed.
He knows he's in the wrong season.
A nurse spoon-feeds him soft food.
Slant snow crosses his eyes. Coyotes circle.

Childhood Westerns

Damn fine woman, my father'd say,
taking in Miss Kitty's
bodice poppin' cleavage,
painted face and nails,
voice gritty as the main street
Marshall Dillon and Festus tumbled into -
Colt 45's drawn for another high noon showdown.

There would have been an accountin'
if it was my old man's furniture
got broke up or bottle of whiskey
shattered agin'st the wall.
I've seen his angle axed hand,
every muscle in his arm flex'd,
the perpetrator hot-footin'
it like a hound dog with its tail
'tween its legs. After the divorce,
he brought red-dyed women home.

My Father Prepares Himself for the Task Ahead

When air reflects sunlight
and my body braces against the cold
I think of my father
a small dot on the white northern landscape
and how he rebuilt downed planes.
How the night before each rescue
he caressed
the blue/black steel of his revolver
with oiled cloths.

How the chambers spun empty
as he told of the relentless dark
howl of wolves, week-long survival whiteouts
in a one man tent.

I watched each calculated turn
each metal click
as he reassembled his weapon
checked the bullets in shining rows.

Look how he cradles the gun
in its soft black leather case.

Piano Lessons

Each week the little girl rides a bus home alone from her piano lessons and takes a short-cut through the graveyard. She traces names and dates with her fingers. Seasons lengthen and shorten shadows. She thinks of the words she reads, the people who wrote them. How the dead don't mind what anyone says. She watches flowers on new graves shrivel and die, plastic ones pale and gather dust. Earth sprouts grass. She always latches the iron gate after her. When they ask, *Are you afraid?* She says, *No. They are just people who are very quiet.*

Bringing in the Cattle

Photography by Kim Taylor
Seasons of Ranching - Fall

By now, the brands have healed.
A cowboy urges the herd
toward winter, low bellows
hollow the burnished landscape.
A sleepy sun deepens wrinkles of shale.

This land carves its ache on white bone,
raw winds fossil beneath layers
before the first snowflake,
before the scrape of glaciers.

Au coeur vaillant rein d'impossible:
Nothing is impossible for a willing heart.

Clouds, soft-edged swords, slice the winter sky, nestle above the
Rockies. Can a mountain not help but reach toward the heavens? Can a
bush not be consumed by fire? Once, my father, piloting his Cessna in
the Rockies, executed a stalled turn, fixed wings lurching bottomless in
my gut. Sweet as cotton candy. Silence. We fell into space.

      Cascade   Mount Rundle   Three Sisters

Eagle nests and cliffs so close an out-stretched hand could touch them.
Cloud filaments tangled around us, through us. Angel wings. Yes!
I painted those moments on the canvas of my mind. Etched our
histories on the face of boulders and clouds. Splattered colours: winter,
summer, fear, happiness. Drought. I wove conversations into the altar
of sky until reality and imagination fused together. Picture the full
moon exposing dreams in daylight as cirrus blind his path. Sometimes
only clouds keep your thoughts.

Innocence
for amm

The children built cities in the sandbox,
old dog lounged among them as towers and mud cakes rose.
And when they came to us from a fall,
we wiped their bloody noses, tweezed gravel from road rash,
salved and bandaged weeping wounds and sent them out again.
We never thought coffin or cremation, brass or silver handle.
Wheat ripened on stalks, autumn currents rustled across the land.
We combined, stacked, and filled the hayloft; fitted a blade
on the tractor and waited, waited in the nativity of sleep
for seed catalogues.

Green tufts sprouted along south exposures.
Crocus bloomed on the edge of snowdrifts,
as if their petals had lavendered the entire winter.
Our dreams were thistle, thorns poking into a gloved night,
healed the instant we awoke.

        And if we found ourselves barefoot in the moonlight
reeling in luminescent sheets, we would pause, laundry basket
against hip, listen to frogs croak their song, watch shadows play
in the silent forest, not even notice that faint stir of leaves
pass before the stillness.

On Visiting the Desert After Learning of a Friend's Lapse into a Coma

Cacti simply exist.
The world a distant breath
beyond the point of a quill.

They have no need to wait.
For what? Sun? Rain?
Thirst?

Machu Picchu

Now the spoiler has come: does it care?
Not faintly. It has all time.
                    Carmel Point, byRobinson Jeffers

        In its own time now, this great city
still and silent as the mountain it is built upon
accepts within its thin air and brilliant light
my footsteps. I tread toward the Sun Gate.

Quartz   serpentine   granite

A language to which I am foreign,
bearing the imprint of each step before me.
Stones fit so tight not even a hair can pass.

Learning to Drive

You needed someone to edge the jeep forward
while you loaded wood on the red trailer,
told me to dress warm and grabbed two pillows
to prop me closer. Gearshift set in first,
you showed me how to release the clutch, inch
forward in that rusty vehicle with plastic windows,
crankcase heavy and stubborn in the cold.
I lurched and stalled more times than forward
and you ballooned the day with expletives
best left for a barroom or brawl. Sunday morning,
snow blinding white, deep over my thighs,
so cold it would freeze a witch's tit, you said
but we stomped through the bush and piled wood
on that trailer, the sun a peculiar brilliant,
peeked through winter branches, watching us,
watching me, eleven years old, fall in love
with gearshifts, wheels, axles and cars.

The Carcass

Silence woke me each time he returned from hunting
out of season. I would slip a jacket over my nightgown
and go to the garage as my father's friends unloaded
their canvas-wrapped carcass from the truck bed.
No words were spoken. The men laid their prize carefully
on the concrete floor and my father slid the garage door
into place. There was a bare minimum light and I stood
in the shadows, shivered as they unrolled their prey.
The kill so clean there was no blood. The silence so large.
Larger than any animal has the right to be. No one
spoke to me. They did not say: *There's school in the*
morning, or *It's 3 am.* The men hoisted the body
on a hook, folded the tarp as neat as a flag and placed
it on its shelf. Suddenly, everyone was gone. Switches
off, doors locked. Men to their cars, my family to bed.
All doors closed soft. Even running water drained quiet.

Nightmare

In every one of these dreams, I am a bull moose
careening through the forest.
I am the little girl who eats the moose
and inhabits the moose's body.
My skin becomes fur,
feet and hands cloven.
Sometimes, I become the hunter.
In my hand, a shiny revolver
as black as night fever.
I pull the hammer back,
press the trigger. A bullet splits hairs,
explodes a heart.
I seek his forgiveness, but he cannot.
His dead eye reflects thunder
and lightning anger.
I am as empty as the magazine.
Spinning, spinning.
As cold as steel.
I am the nightmare. The letters
and words go on and on.
There is no beginning. No end.
The beast circles the forest, the cottage,
the city. He stalks the alley,
ascends the stairs. I hear him every night.
He is the glint behind that leaf, the glass eye
in every shadow. The gun beneath the pillow.

Dreams

She dreams of a man,
his back bent to the earth.
What? What does he plant
along the long, furrowed
row of his thought?
Sometimes, he stands
beside a fence, wires
barbed through sky's
canvas. He fixes his eyes
on golden wheat sunsets,
lines etching long into his
deep face, as long as any journey
could be. There are no
border dogs in her dreams.
Horses sometimes gallop
down main street. Wild
horses. This man's bones
have been written on clouds
for decades. So many
stories this dream could be
a painting. Layer upon
layer upon layer. Oils,
pastels, charcoal, chalk.
Can dreams be pleated
into reality? Is there even
a place to walk his dog?

Seasons

Suddenly, it is winter.
Just yesterday afternoon,
I knelt to the ground
planted daffodils and narcissus,
sun a weak warmth on my shoulders.
I worried the squirrel chittering
on a spruce bough will
steal my bulbs. Now, this morning,
weighted white covers
my knee dents in the earth.
Patio glass squiggled in frost.
Garden and lawn silenced.
Clouds genuflect to earth
and earth strains toward
falling snow. The squirrel
is gone. I wonder if
my garden misses me,
my thundered footsteps,
heart pulses or breath
as I dug and pruned
all summer and fall,
or if it understands
this beginning and end,
before and above us.
How overnight
the long dark has begun.
The great leveler.

Midnight Run

I remember you best in late fall after a midnight run setting nets.
We filleted fish on plywood balanced between sawhorses. Six,
ten, fourteen years old. All those years, hands and wrists covered
in numbing fish guts and you, deep frying by the porch, rye and
7-Up in one hand called to Mom for more batter. Flood lights
filled the yard as if it were noon, moths flirted crazy. Our breath
a light frost. The world fanned out in phantoms just beyond that
circle of light. Ghost trees, bush shadows. Muted coyotes, small
animal rustle. You looked so happy. You laughed and raised your
drink, then another one and, *another for the road,* you quipped,
edging closer and closer to that wilderness. Almost. Almost, as if
you were begging to be caught.

My Father As Tsar 1946

Kingsway Avenue, south of the Municipal Airport.
My father, a young man, contemplates his future as he paces.

In khakis and leather fly-jacket, he pauses beneath a street light.
Shields a match strike, lights a smoke, heads west.

Exhaling a cloud of smoke, snow, knife sharp, pummels his body.
Blue runway lights blur, he zippers against the cold, turns east.

Flight boots worn and thin, he continues, without losing step.
Sinew and muscle, a one-man phalanx, he turns and marches west.

He raises his collar and with no hat, sets his face into the wind.
Daring the elements, just daring them to ground him, he turns east.

Waiting

This is the curb, where, for a Coke
and chocolate bar, I learned to wait
while my parents went in for a cold brew.
Spruce Grove, Entwhistle, Wildwood, Hinton.
Leaning into the shade of the left front fender.
Even then, I didn't like the sun or heat of the car.
I have been here a long time.
People enter and leave.
Smoke billows through the doors.
My bum is numb, eyes sore from the book propped on my knees.
A lot of dead bugs splattered on chrome.
Usually, it is mid-afternoon or early evening.
But even then, men congregate, butt their smokes
on the sidewalk or flick them between cars.
I think I am invisible. The men are mostly native
and I am not allowed to talk to anyone.

A few years later, in grade seven, I learn about Residential
Schools when Sister LaForce comes to our school from a
northern Mission. But today there is just the men and me.
I sidle closer to the car or go to the driver's door my father left
unlocked and crank the window down an inch or two, lock the
car from the inside.

There Are No Stories In My Family

I arrived when life was looking easy, war over,
three kids in school, mortgage rate low.
Buick paid for in cash. A mistake,
a surprise; my sister said I cried all the time,
my crib in the hall. Maybe it was time
to move anyhow. A little girl, I longed
to be part of their past, the Twenties,
Dirty Thirties, World War II, and grew up
sifting through their ash, always afraid;
shadows, sirens. Once, after a bad dream,
my father called me silly and I looked
at the colourless cinders in my palm,
felt the grit and decided to turn
my hand over and let it all fall.

The night my mother died...

the rear end of a car travelled down a highway in the closing
scene of a motel movie. *Amazing Grace* played and credits rolled
and rolled. I dozed beside sleep, my day a replay swabbing puce
mucus from Mom's mouth. Green-sponged Q-tips. The squelch,
the sea, the spill of it across the sheets, onto floor, down hospital
halls, into streets, the slick trailing to my room. Startled, I bolt
into the silence, chasing a 4 am digital clock. My heart quickens,
I listen to my breath, the depth and aloneness of each tiny intake,
but blanket warmth soothes me and I snuggle into deep slumber,
without dream. When sun rays open my eyes past my promised
return, there was no need to rush.

Summoning

Please come before winter.

Before north winds crumple veined leaves to the ground and prairie grass is laid by snow.

Before river's rage slows to a trickle between ice floes or low clouds obscure landscape and snow muffles earth.

Please come before frost snaps limbs or yellow birdsong is erased by this season.

Please come before the absence of light weighs on me.

Please.

My Mother's Sister

Talked non-stop, in the same language she wrote to my mother.
A calligraphy of curves and loops, lines and circles, written on
two sides of blue vellum air-mail paper that crinkled when read.
Intricate as the nets she made for Russian fishermen during
the Cold War. Her voice, soft and even, like the metronome on
our piano, seeped through the whole house as she sat in the
living room or kitchen, cigarette smoke, a thick pencil, rose
above endless cups of coffee. She talked gauge and shuttles, her
nets knit intimately as a sweater for a husband or lover. She
talked of her husband dying, she talked of death as if it was a
friend, her words undulating, a drowned man's hair in
underwater currents. She never came up for air. She invited
shadows that needed to be forgotten into our house, into our lives.

White Chalk on Slate

Sometimes when I glance over my shoulder, I glimpse Sister La Force, white wrists exposed, as she nests her hand on the back of Alex Swann's neck and guides him to the Principal's office, her frame draped in black, rosary buried in folds. A crazy penguin, he called her and now stumbles along beside this gliding nun, head hung in contrition, even from a sixty-year distance, a perceptible sneer. Back and forth, up and down, warm fabric brushed us as the sisters and mothers bent to help or answer a question. This looking back, like a night wind. White chalk on slate. Erased. Mother Xavier storms her tall, lank frame into Hamlet's lines. Black ghosts extracting our best. Chem 20, Mother Kevin, sleeves hiked to her elbows, bird tiny, set test tubes in the rack. Winter-blue irises. Too pretty to be a nun we all said and soon she left. Our vision, drawn past the habit's black, past the white wimple to their face. Their eyes. The wells of their pupils.

The Rosary

My father knew how lips moved without sound, the click of his mother's beads from the womb. He watched each day as she filled the kerosene lamp set before the Blessed Mary's statue, felt her soft breath extinguish the taper after she lit the wick. Knelt beside her as a child. In the late thirties he installed electricty and changed incandescent bulbs for her. But the benediciton did not change. He knew each prayer she recited as he knew his own face and hands. As he knew his flight plans, spin of a revolver magazine. A woman's body. He knew each word and their order. He knew confession and penance and vows. He knew it all. In French and English.

The Gospel

At the cottage, late morning fire crackles.
October chill. Bacon and eggs sizzle,
coffee percolates on the wood heater.
On my lap, *A Tree Grows in Brooklyn.*
Pages turn slow. Sunday.
No church today, Mom says,
we are closer to God in silence.
Dad at the kitchen table sips
a beer and juice.

What was that Gospel? Tap, tap, tap.
Sister LaForce asks Monday morning
and stands me in front of my grade
seven class. Tap, tap, tap. Black boots
poke from beneath her habit, yardstick
clicking against her leg. Tap, tap, tap.
Again and again and again she asks.
Her voice marches to the back of the class,
strikes the ceiling. Tap, tap, tap.
My eyes meet hers. *I don't know.*

*I was at home reading my father's
Playboy magazine.*
There is no air. Only silence. Heavy
and light at the same time.

Seba Beach

for John

At the lake it was just my brother and me, like the autumn I was
seven, building a fort. Only us in the wide breath of forest. We
packed hammer, nails, saw and stray boards and began nailing
between trees. We dragged long branches and plugged the spaces
between, layered leaves on the floor. Our voices filled the thin
air, footsteps crunched. By mid-afternoon we shed jackets and
unwrapped peanut butter and jam sandwiches and Cokes.
Maybe a McIntosh apple. We lazed on our leaf floor and he
talked and talked and talked of all he knew. It was so quiet, just
his voice, the blue lake before us. The sun beat long shadows
between branches. The whole world just him and me. It was the
now and we fit into that day in our little fort, his twelve-year-old
voice filled the warm air, his words tucked into me like a blanket.

There Are No Stories In My Family

The young woman leans over a window box.
A soldier stretches to kiss her. Between them,
yellow flowers blossom. Marigolds.
France. 1942. His bike leans against the house.
Within a week he ships out. Atlantic Ocean.
Torpedoes. U-boats lap the margins of his letters.
Days brindled in fear. She walks ripened October,
a summer promise in each step. Let's say
there were six witnesses in organza and lace,
dark suits and wide ties. Black and white portrait,
framed in stained oak. They bought into the stock
of borders that never fade or turn sepia. There were
anniversaries, birthdays, Christmas. For years
there was a New Year. Then it ended.

The Forgetting
for Fedora

Tell her,

       now I understand the Nor'wester she spoke of,
walking tethered on an ice-coated battleship in the middle of a
North Atlantic winter.

Tell her,
       I understand the importance of silk stockings while
fighting a war and keeping the seams straight.

Tell her,
       I always hear the silence in Trafalgar Square on D-Day
through her ears.

Tell her,
       I have attempted to carry it all with grace. A quiet
grace. Not allow the pummel and wail to enter.

Tell her,
       soon. Soon, I too will stand in line and wait at the end
of the day for my shot of rum.

Beginning the End

Eighty-seven years old and my mother still canned peaches and
brought in her garden as if she was a young woman, like the
summer I was six and she asked me to chop off carrot tops.

My left pointer finger ... slips beneath the knife.
She settles me on the back step,
blood soaking through the tightly bound facecloth
weeping red drops on the concrete,
mother determined we wait the hours
for Dad to come home.

I turn away as the doctor freezes and stitches
hanging skin. Dad's whiskey breath louder
than the antiseptic.

All that fall, between blackberry and raspberry jam, she played
Euchre with the Seba Seniors, bringing a serve-twenty pasta
casserole each week for pot luck. A bad chest cold kept her home
New Year's and by January 23rd, pain gripping her lungs, an
ambulance rushed her to emergency. Exhausted and on the edge
of medicated sleep, she was sent home. Flaming shadows
spooked her. A fire in the garage, mauling the interior, billowing
smoke into the frosted air! The night scourged and shattered.

just as my cries did years ago
when the anesthetic lost its grip on my finger.
Pain, clawing up my arm.

Now, fifty years later, she rises. The steel cylinder of her next
breath trails behind as she coughs pneumonia and dials 911
the second time that night.

On Her Eighty-Eighth Birthday, My Mother Asks Me to Iron

After The Shirt, *by Robert Pinsky*

She draws the Ventolin deep
and I can see she lacks a strength
that was there just last week.
As the sofa accepts her fraility,
she asks me to iron her blouse.
The deft lift. The heat. The steam.
A ritual performed without thought.
The collar. The placket. The sleeves.
Pressed on a flannel sheet, pinned beneath.
The cuffs. The front. The back.
A March sun sways shadows through the room,
our talk small and quiet.
The garment. The cotton. The weave.
The memory of white.

Meditation on Wasps

The air strains with wasps as they siphon nectar from Mountain Ash berries. For some, the end of their short life draws near, others are still being born. A few will survive until spring. The week before my mother died, she discussed hockey with my husband and son. Breath shallow, she struggled for each word. Her body a shadow beneath green sheets. Yet she wondered how my son's hockey team was doing, his right winger role, the small Saskatchewan teams in his league. She wanted to know, *how do players get away with outrageous salaries when they don't perform?* Despite the odds, their incessant hum and quest for food remains constant. Back and forth between paper and tree their tireless little bodies vibrate. Each a beat of wing and heart.

Abduction

Not one thing that hot day cared,
traffic floated through asphalt heat waves,
people ordered take-out.
Believe me, I speak the truth,
clouds continued to shade,
a breeze played its music across the prairie.
Later, a walk away, her little body
among the tallest prairie grass.
There is no comfort here, in this funeral home.
The rosary laced through her fingers,
eyes sleeping, the white dress.
Each flower a hand's span.
Each stem plucked from the earth.
Here, we are all strangers, separated
by death pains and dusty roads,
quiet about the wrongs in our lives.
But now is not the time for silence.
We must be lions, tigers, hunters,
prowl into that night, alert our watchers,
so whoever did this will not be folded back
into the safety of us only remembering.

Remembrance Day

On the kitchen table, breakfast things.
An open newspaper.
List of soldiers killed in Afghanistan,
some names the same as my family:
Phillip, Richard, Anthony, John.
I think of their wives, children, parents,
waiting on a tarmac somewhere.
Fumes and engines assault their senses.
The dreaded moment as the belly
of a Hercules opens
and shrouded coffins emerge.

    I walk to my garden, nudge
stray branches and leaves from my path,
pick up a gum wrapper, a lost flyer.
I wonder at this day that could be anyone's last.
Bouquets that lay a loved one to rest,
wreaths that remember.

    It feels good to stand here on this threshold of ordinary.
Chickadees and sparrows chirp in the cotoneaster,
tulip bulbs asleep in the ground,
bone meal cultivated around each plant,
leaves raked, orange garbage bags beside the curb.
I tilt my face toward the sun, the same light that shines
on the other side of the world.

The Last Afternoon of My Mother's Life

I cannot stop touching her.

I sponge her forehead,
cheeks and neck,
bloated stomach,
massage her moon-white legs.

Propped between pillows,
she labours with each breath,
drifts in and out,
gasps for words
between oxygen puffs.

I stroke the length
of her arms,
follow her blue veins
beneath translucent skin,
in and out I breathe her,

match the life lines
of our palms,
weave our fingers
together.

Meanook Cemetery

We are burying our mother, facing south where the sun will stretch its fingers across the marble stone each morning and illuminate her name. She will sleep among the farmhouses and pastures she walked as a child. But today, a rain squall ushers us beneath a rusted arch onto a muddy trail that leads to her grave. Sunny in the city when we left, I wore the wrong clothes and duck beneath my brother's umbrella, straw hat soaked. Wet dribbles down my back. A crazy wind flaps the Pastor's prayers and hymns around our huddled circle, pushes into the small of our backs, and shepherds us, yes, shepherds us closer and closer.

May First

Driving home along Crowchild Trail
burdened with traffic and clouds,
I realize, I have let your death date slip by.
Is it eight or nine years?
A rip in the clouds allows the sun to throw
purple light to earth.
I came early that day but you left before dawn.
Your body beneath green sheets.
Small, white, still.
The oxygen machine silenced for the first time
in five years. I stood beside your bed
in the pink morning of your room,
both of us gloved in our separate silence.
Ten, twenty, thirty minutes until your husband arrived.
It was his birthday, wasn't it?

After the Funeral

This evening, after the funeral, a yellow butterfly lights on my arm, clings to the fine hairs and stays while I make my way from flowerbed to flowerbed. This insect seeking what? Warmth? He stays in this silence and I think of Batoche, when a friend's ashes were given back to the earth, a butterfly lingered as hymns of the land welcomed a daughter home. Last autumn, in a narrow sunless street of old Rome, a Monarch floated from one ancient stone to another, then landed on the fake ivy outside a shop. Now this little epistle pleats its bright wings slowly in and out, in and out, on my arm.

Ordinary

After *Kindness* by Naomi Shihab Nye

Before you know what ordinary is, you must visit a funeral home
and view the body of a friend you made plans with just a few
days before. You must watch as the people dearest to you, buried
beneath flowers, sympathy cards and lasagne casseroles, have
their mother's urn pressed into their hands. You must stand in
their home and see the unmade bed and laundry still scattered
on the floor. Then you must hug and kiss good-bye, turn the key
in your car and drive home less than a week after the phone call
and discover that milk and bread still line grocery store shelves,
traffic lights change green, yellow, red. Your dog needs grooming.
You step into the rain, walk through the neighbourhood,
past the church. Yellow parking lines gleam wet, your dog busy
on new grass and then look you look up as an SUV pulls
alongside and see the smiling face of Vivian, who you haven't
seen in six months. She rolls down her window and you pick up
your wet dog, hold him as he shivers beneath your jacket. Your
feet sink into the soft earth as you walk across the boulevard and
then you stand in the rain as the city hums around you, and
become one of two women talking in the quiet of a road.

A Measure of Taste

More and more you turn toward your childhood;
the slide and snap of metal
as your father cleans his rifle after the hunt
and tells you how Marie sent a jar of pickles.
You wonder, with four carcasses hung,
empty whiskey and beer cases stacked in the garage,
how pickles are memorable.
Now, you measure your life,
warm bread and butter after school,
Chardonnay in a hot tub after cross-country skiing,
taste of egg salad sandwiches at your mother's funeral.
How emptiness catches in your throat
as you sip tea at your mother's vacant table.

      Think of Eve, breath labored, body grained
in sweat. Cool air sifts smooth on her skin. Branches
bow before her. The weight of fruit in her palm.
A crunch.

Monopoly

It was my brother's game
He was the one who counted
And I, seven years younger
The one who hid.
                    Lorna Crozier

At twelve years old, my brother and his friends
didn't play hide and seek, cowboys and Indians,
cops and robbers. Instead, they chose tokens
and tossed dice. Through long summer after-
noons and northern half-nights, they occupied
the family veranda. Peanut butter and jam
on bread. Dubble Bubble. Six-cent popsicles,
wooden sticks chewed razor thin in nervous strain.
Blood beat loud through young veins.
It was my brother's game.

Rescued from the back lane trash, play money
torn and stained, board scratched and pocked.
Favourite milk token lost. Tempers flared
over die stuck on brittled Scotch tape strung
across center fold. Community Chest and Chance
cards mangy and rough as an old groundhog,
half of them missing. Get Out of Jail Free
edge worn thin. My brother insisted
he be banker, it was the game he found.
He was the one who counted

money and managed property. One game
could last for days, buying and selling
properties. quiet deals between food and sleep.
They experienced wealth and bankruptcy,
developed a capitalistic hunger
upgrading to red hotels from green houses.
Woe to anyone who touched their game,
or treat cache under the sofa. They played
through heat, wind, rain, lightning, thunder.
And I, seven years younger,

was always a side glance away, ready
to bring Kool-Aid or cookies and once they
asked me to fill in for a winning boy.
I took his chair and blew for luck.
Park Place. Baltic Avenue. States Avenue.
Home. Breathe. Next turn Atlantic. Two hotels.
Then Pacific. His empire gone.
His anger scattered board and table.
He didn't understand, I was just a kid.
The one who hid.

Lady Luck

Kept late hours with my childhood. Buxom redhead from the Old West, she heaped her hair high, tendrils curled down her neck. Magenta eyelids, gushing breasts. I invoked her touch, her grace, with each turn of the die or card. Around the table, small smirks exposed behind curling cigarette smoke. Jim and Neil winked at me, Dad's rumbled chuckle, Mom's eyes aware of my every nuance. Lorette and Betty thrummed the tabletop with their long, red nails. I shuffled cards for hours, dealt an empty table, the deck cut brisk and sharp. I dreamt in diamonds, clubs, spades and hearts. Trump and tricks. Knowing each deal unpredictable. I learned Lady Luck was not a guardian angel, she could bring down all the kings and queens, jacks and jokers. I heard her standing over us. Taunting. Teasing. The good cards buried in the discard pile. Suits of regret we willingly wore.

He is driving...

a Chrysler, Jeep, construction truck or
we are tramping through bush.
Winter, autumn. Never summer. This dream.
He is gone now, but I speak of the time
he had no voice. When his thoughts were
coyote, wolf, deer. You understand
with a person such as this, it is difficult
to speak ordinary. To speak of Buddha's
10,000 things, a teenage zit or nuns
who do not allow sleeveless dresses.
Conversation was defined within paw prints,
rabbit snare, guns. *That rifle has quite
the kickback, hold it away from your shoulder.
Here, rest the barrel on this log.*

In the church basement after a funeral,
I spoke aloud he should not smoke
with his son who had throat cancer
and walked away. A handsome man
in black suit, thin tie, he sat there
drawing on his cigarette. In this dream
he laughs and sucks his smoke again
and again, exhales smoke rings, bullets,
turns and walks away. He leaves no
footprints or bent branches. He leaves
no trail.

Caterpillars

There are some stories you never forget.

My father knew bread lines and scuffed shoes from the Salvation
Army.
       He knew crops that laid down in fields and cried.
He saw paths and roads disappear beneath drifting soil.
       He knew fighter planes and bombs.
But he told stories of how tent caterpillars derailed trains,
       the buckle and bend of an iron beast
as it braked along black, crawling rails.
       Cars fell to their sides like toys.

A little girl, I walked the railway tracks five miles to Wabamun
       for a chocolate bar and Coke,
fat wasps rose from creosote to the warm, sweet bottle neck.
       I hopped from tie to tie, stepped calmly into the ditch
as the train lumbered past, every detail of my father's story
       engraved on the back of my eyes.

First the steel lines begin to vibrate, then the engine
       comes into sight, small then larger and larger.
I placed a penny on the track,
       before the smokestack wisps smoke,
before the caterpillars began their march,
       before I slipped into the ditch.

In another world, there were soup kitchens
                    where hobos and families queued together.
There were warm days and cold. Roads disappeared
                    beneath drifitng soil and snow.
Caterpillars derailed trains. Crops laid down in fields
                    and cried.
War came. Clouds scudded across the country;
                    armed, tinged with blood.
Children roamed free, observed their parents' battles
                    from mountain tops, as if filming a movie
or as God watching. It was easier that way.

Think of the sunlight on your face,
  its ancient path
 folding the wilderness within.

Acknowledgements

To my family, with gratitude, for all their love and support, this book could not be written without you: Richard, Stacey, Tim, Laura, Leon, Julie, Anthony, Heather, Chad, David and Lexie.

Thanks to Kate Reid for her unwavering interest and friendship.

The seeds of this book took root at the Banff Writing Studio 2010 with the guidance and expertise of Don McKay, Stephanie Bolster and John Glenday. Thank you and thanks to all the alumni.

Thanks to Richard Harrison, mentor and friend whose insight and editing was instrumental in developing this collection. Thanks also to Rosemary Griebel, Juleta Severson-Baker, Bob Stallworthy and Chris Dodd for their ongoing wisdom and poetic guidance and to the Thursday Night Poetry Group for their commitment to poetry in finding *the best words in the best order*.

A special thanks to Micheline Maylor for her intelligence, perceptiveness and sensitivity that she has been so generous to share as this book took shape over the past three years.

Joan Shillington is a Calgary poet and has been published in *The Antigonish Review, Fiddlehead, Grain, Prairie Fire* and *Freefall Magazine* as well as four anthologies. She has won various contests over the years.

She is currently a poetry editor for *Freefall Magazine.*

Joan's first book of poetry, *Revolutions,* was published by Leaf Press (2008).